Spare and lush, Myung Mi Kim's *Civil Bound* is a "sight  embled heart markers. Her quicksilver connections, reformula ___ obilize the possible and impossible moves. Like subtitles of re ___ s, with her passages of diagonal bars and a cross of verticals, ___ titutes language as we see and hear it. The sites are, among ___ ankers, canals, ledgers from the Carlisle Indian school, froz ___ , liver broth. Just the phrase "liver broth" (indicating contamination in water) sings and singles out the logics of domination. Kim quotes from Theodore Roosevelt's Letter to the President of the American Defense Society from 1919, there is "room for but one language here." Does her use of the word "traduction" mean "slander, defame" (English) or "translation" (French) or both? A call, a cry, a burial site and a tribute to fathers and mothers, *Civil Bound* is a stunning book. Prepare to be stunned.

NORMA COLE, AUTHOR OF *FATE NEWS*

A 1913 article on the construction of the Panama Canal opens by marveling at "the unlimited audacity of man in ripping open the mountains [and] penetrating the jungles in an effort to throw two greatest oceans together" and continues to herald this "greatest assault ever made upon nature" as also the "greatest of all monuments of marching civilization." The title of Myung Mi Kim's scrupulously expansive long poem, *Civil Bound*, registers both the blind hubris of this civilizing mission or what she calls "hemispheric lust" and the binds of a language system that can be marshalled towards such a determined disavowal of its many human and environmental casualties. Kim recasts her abiding re-membering of the history of Korea's colonization and diaspora in her first volume, *Under Flag*, but here enfolds it into a broader and more assiduous reckoning with what it means to be a citizen and a civil subject of the US, especially in these times of a resurgent nationalism and xenophobia.

LAURA HYUN YI KANG, AUTHOR OF *COMPOSITIONAL SUBJECTS*

Precision is a lyricism all its own. Austerity has nothing to do with it. Every page is full. There's room for many languages, especially in telling the reduction to one. The largesse is obvious, mysteriously stark, and interminable, endlessly diverse, like what flows before, and then after, a river, hard in its erosions and redactions. Having found a sonic niche of her own, Myung Mi Kim is our species, or gives us as close to a reason as we've got.

FRED MOTEN, AUTHOR OF *CONSENT NOT TO BE A SINGLE BEING*

Even if you know Myung Mi Kim's alchemically original sense of time and sound—what comes through the "tattered conduit of jawbone and ear" (the precision of her labor with words . . . how she represents writing as arrangement), remain open to being shaken by the surprising and ever economical force of this book. Beginning with a growl rising up out of oceanic space, *Civil Bound* leads the reader to think (in the way Myung leads through pauses and meditation upon the progression of words and phrases as inventions) each poem as a durational action that re-animates, re-constitutes history—history, violently breaking the human world into two parts ("scolding wings removed   cuts flushed"), civilized and savage. Myung Mi Kim's deep sense of what language does and can do in service or opposition to history is simply unparalleled.

SIMONE WHITE, AUTHOR OF *DEAR ANGEL OF DEATH*

Myung Mi Kim's *Civil Bound* is a breathtaking book of canals composed of air and water and land, of bodies, of labor and power. Within its networks of human meaning, one witnesses the violent incursions of colonialism upon physical and cultural geographies and ecosystems, including patterns of bondage created under the guise of civilization. But that's just one of the refracted meanings of *Civil Bound*. The space within these poems is full of open questions. By what social contracts are we bound? Toward what outcomes are we bound? What binds us together? Of what are we made? Kim's attention to overarching systems and their patterns of interference generates a deeper understanding—and affirmation—of mutuality and relation that is as resilient as the air that passes through these profoundly moving poems.

ELIZABETH WILLIS, AUTHOR OF *ALIVE: NEW AND SELECTED POEMS*

civil bound

also by Myung Mi Kim

Under Flag (Kelsey Street Press, 1991)
The Bounty (Chax Press, 1996)
Dura (Sun & Moon Press, 1999)
Spelt (with Susan Gevirtz, a+bend press, 2000)
Commons (University of California Press, 2002)
River Antes (Atticus/Finch, 2006)
Penury (Omnidawn Publishing, 2009)

civil bound

OMNIDAWN PUBLISHING
OAKLAND, CALIFORNIA
2019

myung mi kim

Cover art by Amy Trachtenberg
Double take, 2019
32 x 45 inches
pigment print on rag paper mounted on linen
Photo credit Dennis Letbetter

Cover and interior set in Octavian MT Std and Perpetua Std

Cover and interior design by Gillian Olivia Blythe Hamel

Printed in the United States
by Books International, Dulles, Virginia
On 55# Glatfelter B19 Antique
Acid Free Archival Quality Recycled Paper

Library of Congress Cataloging-in-Publication Data

Names: Kim, Myung Mi, 1957- author.
Title: Civil bound / Myung Mi Kim.
Description: Oakland, California : Omnidawn, 2019.
Identifiers: LCCN 2019014947 | ISBN 9781632430717 (paperback)
Subjects: | BISAC: POETRY / General. | POETRY / American / Asian American.
Classification: LCC PS3561.I414 A6 2019 | DDC 811/.54--dc23
LC record available at https://lccn.loc.gov/2019014947

Published by Omnidawn Publishing, Oakland, California
www.omnidawn.com   (510) 237-5472   (800) 792-4957
10 9 8 7 6 5 4 3 2 1
ISBN: 978-1-63243-071-7

Sue Bok Kim
(1924-2016)

the oceans held up a snarling dog

eardrum bramble

salty necks, heaven hung

an according bargain

short luck's business

limbs or lives   horns together

savagery's judge

not in the codices or chants

charity kin, hair and lime burrowed

arches | vermillion

platform of moveable objects

for live spectacle

arch of armaments and charts

stronghold | prowess

a link of people sorted—size, strength, age

bellflower broth, liver broth

hemispheric lust

flowing campaign

apropos the financier's stride

charmed forgery

talon of contagion, in receipt

well placed towers

glowing colts

thrown down the wells

scoured off the foundation

corruption balked before alms

boulders, mechanical parts, or persons

pledged to asunder

humble rules for eyes and fingers

errant convalescence

by arms and legs fettered

by the wallets of tongues

taught to make coffins for each other

in the museum of Public Actions

in the tone of guides, "sacred place"

fence around the burial site   the leaf blower

It is conceded that an interoceanic canal through any of the isthmus passes of the western hemisphere is a necessity for the present and prospective commerce of the world.

1872

sounds produced by using air from the lungs

if the air is pushed out

if the air is sucked in

scolding wings removed   cuts flushed

choke canal

abuts agricultural sunken medical

1 pair gloves

3 yds calico

whiskey

crackers

watch guard

1 deck cards

The Settlers Ledger
Ft. Union, NM
1863

e t n w e t h g d a a
x h l h d t a e r u a
p a y o e n e g l h
r t s s d o n t h l a
e i t e t o f t h t y
s t n h a t u e e h t
s h e t t o r t r i e
e e t r u e h p s n r
d h e i s s o e r u
i e t t w i n a p
v n i i g u n g s m e
e d e s o o d r i t e o
r i n n v y v e n h r p
y a g n e e a g e i l
n l o i r a r t c e
d s i t s n n n e n e a
e s m y a s a n o
c s h a p e c t t g i f
i h n a n o u i l s
d o l i t t l m o i a
e u a i d h a o n s g l
d l n n w e r s a h o l
l d g d b h r t l o
y u i y o t i l d r
b a a l h p t a a
t e g n t i a e o i n e c
h e h s n w e g n e
e t p e g l e s u o s
a o u p u a r a u
i u p u e a n f u g g 1
d g i n r g g u n e h 8
e h l i m e u l d 8
a t t i a e a f 6
t a s o r e
t

from atlas bulbs a skull grows

f *t* *nr*

rift immunology

cut from hoof or fingerprint

packed off vessels, hollow

larynx and feral irritants

effacement of oh father, mother, the, we

pity doves

silicate

the Great Lakes

silt   slit   syllabaries

ob   /a   s/r

traduction

fin and aspen grove

persons to appear
persons who made

debris architecture

if a species cannot find a sonic niche of its own, it will not survive

circumpolar

rifles at the ready, aimed

next to

distribution of ground corn

```
r     e  f  d  o
o  a     o  i  u
o  n  i  r  f  n
m  d  t  t  f  t
      u     e  r
f  t  w  n  r  y
o  h  o  e  e
r  a  u        n  1
   t  l  b  c  9
b     d  u  e  1
u  i     t  s  7
t  s  b
      e  a  o
o  t           f
n  h  n  c
e  e  o  r  l
   t  i     a
l  e     m  n
a  n  m  e  g
n  g  e     u
g  l  r  t  a
u  i  e  o  g
a  s  l     e
g  h  y  p
e     e  i
   l  a  r  n
h  a     p
e  n  m  e  t
r  g  i  t  h
e  u  s  u  i
   a     a  s
   g     t
      e  c
```

what could not be determined as a dead seagull or feathered driftwood

| |

in _____ days we will reach land

sound like blowing over the mouth of an empty bottle: amphoric

bleating voice sound: egophony

sound of liquid: hyguechema

splashing sound: clapotement

through a column of water: hydrophony

distant transmission of speech: pectoriloquy

```
    w       a r d t a g a g t s m a w n
  i i   c   n e s h   i s i h e o n i k
  n t d o a d s t   w n i n e r t   n f
  s n e u     o   t o e l e   v o w d o
  p e a n p a r o h n e y e n e r a s r
  i s t t l   t f e d r   r e       v   d
  r s h r a v       e i i s a a p e d
  i   r y c e r d p r n m   r n o s r
  n t i   e r i i a f g a a     d w
  g h d c   i g s n u   g t f   e a 1
    i d h o t h e a l a i t u u r n 9
  s s e a f a t a m   n n e t t   d 1
  i   n n   b   s a f d e m u i o     3
  g u   g b l i e   e       p r l f t
  h n t e e e n   c a w c t e i   h j
  t s r d a     a a t e i i   z t e o
    e o   u h t n n     v n t e h   h
  t e p i t e h d a o c i g o   e t n
  o m i n y a e   l f a l     t   r
    l c t   l   d   n   i c h o a l
    y a o   t m e i e   e n o e c d a
    l     h i a s n e n   n   e e
```

quarry   rend

the body of unripe strawberry

profusion of red dirt

on windowsills exposed skin creeping shrubs

Mississippi River   someone has caught a swordfish at the dam   behemoth

many people help to pull it up to the pier

[Talihina / Yankton]
for solo gayageum

owls threaded among dogwoods   a backlit forum

how precisely and how raggedly water erodes the doorjamb

bowl of landowner poison said:
the oxen must be considered in one cluck

[Worksong for Ablation]

shoals adjudicate a mausoleum

| |

what is the progeny of renegade topos

| |

frozen ground refuses the headstone

forest floor desiccated | |

a flung injury | |

initialized equator | |

arborization fish biomass mammal biomass (livestock, humans, wild mammals)

infirm to the ground rituals performed in abeyance aperture splice

fifteen to a stretcher and fiber optics dissemination of warheads limbic accentual

| | compliance ugly

| | pathogenic microbes

| | sinew ferns

compressed air drills | |

dynamite, dredger | |

uploaders, shovels with dippers | |

arbitrariness intermittence with which the gates to the safety zone open votg

tanktainer hoyer evergreen hoyer itawa ttx triton k-line phosphorous intersexed

species vestigial faces on stone pillars pig iron head wounds slick

| | both the canopy and the understory

| | backs swerved, unnatural bow

| | half hour clocks bray

remove 268 million cubic yards of earth | |

                                            | |

abjure mouths | |

intercellular herding of must clear forests and cultivate these in the

_____ manner eyes seeking protection divested of proximity

corpuscle capillary fermata forced migration scriptorium pocked blasted

| | willed geography

| |

| | cut off long hair, forbid native language

||

reprieve ledger ashen ||

||

Korean classroom, 1934
"King Lear' and "Cordelia" written on the board in Japanese

| | isolated sepal

| |

| | the pitch of surveillance

by immolation by pestilence | |

| |

in _____ days we will reach shore | |

enter among rustling plastic edicts batten the seal of sums cyclic

drones subsidiary concentrated into fewer and fewer languages dilation or

distention of a hollow organ cultural transmission involution fray

| | Hello, in America, Fish English

| |

| | level of detail afforded by asphyxia

torsion | |

| |

were to lungs filled with sea | |

Musicale
by the
Carlisle Indian Band and Girls' Mandolin Club
under the direction of Mr. Claude M. Stauffer
Wednesday Evening, April first, Nineteen Eight

Seven thirty   In the Auditorium

Program

卍

Part I

1.	March	Powhatan's Daughter	-	Sousa
2.	Overture	The Merry Wives of Windsor	-	Nicolai
3.	Romance	Souvenirs and Regrets		Beaumont
4.	Excerpts	The Free Lance	-	Sousa
5.	Native	Indian Medicine Dance	-	Bellstedt

Intermission

Program

卐

Part II

6. Characteristic March	White Crow	- - -	Eno
	Girls' Mandolin Club		
7. Overture	The Bronze Horse	- -	Auber
8. Salon Piece	First Heart Throbs	- -	Eilenberg
9. Selection	The Merry Widow	- -	Lehar
10. Humoresque	The Girl I Left Behind Me	- -	Bellstedt
	Star Spangled Banner		

grief ganglion | |

clemency trumpets mute | |

the idea of forgetting when a person is unspecified not specified etymon dried

cornstalks in a semi-circle are walls english proficiency citizenship

life in _____ test civilizing mission property in severalty

| | prolapsed sensorium

a wreath of warblers

pronunciation key for suffering   /abrə'gāSH(ə)n/

all newcomers must newcomers must cinder wages smell of camphor and plaster

dust residual projectile decibel atrophy preceding sunlight if

the chronoscope chronometer coroner if hands

were woven burnholes

yi so ri

flagrant masks carved and inverted

leaching

| | razed burdock

in the form of interdictions

smother cymbals

tattered conduit of jawbone and ear

stone knives in murky liquid

receding immunity

carrion energy grids

what is it   presented by the underbelly of moths

what is   a mutual duration

acetone femurs | |

amplitude [shelled open]

inexorably ignorance

locution cauterized | |

blast radius | | skeletonized rites

the habitable excised
the hospitable excised

[worksong for ablation]

a whetstone

trying at pitch

from defective articulation: alalia

with confusion of words: paraphrasia

from defective intellection: alogia

of motor origin: aphemia

with inability to read: paralexia

with inability to write: paragraphia

| | how a swallow is achieved

greenish violet tinge   her lips

untethered island

bare rigging

congregates

pain's adoration

accept of these waters

swallowed villages   basins of mountains   wicksand   fernbridge

cervical vertebrae and acacias

Great Lakes Stations

Port Washington, WI   1930-1981
Duluth, MN   1939-1981
Chicago, IL   1933-1978
Buffalo, NY   1935-1978
Rogers City, MI   1922-1987
Lorain, OH   1933-1981

habitation   wooden crates in a nameless territory

dented objects for gathering water

plastic footwear two sizes too small   how the cracked heels hang over

the vine suggests sweet potato but notice the cradle of thorns skiff ferry   militarized

eradication's resourcefulness speaking in a prestige language

jaundice shade of bombardment
singed skin grapheme

between ribs   what might be shale

ramshackle peony
meridian bit in the mouth

accept of these waters

lava tubes   tulips   feast days

morning pheasants   anjeonhae

hulls of rice blown free

e s n m   i∧   ys g^   pp^a ^

a ^j   k`^hh^^

b ` `

mercy

the inviolable

for my father and mother

accept of these waters

white-naped crane   red-crowned crane

p. 22
R. W. Shufeldt, "Reports of Explorations and Surveys to Ascertain the Practicality of a Ship-Canal between the Atlantic and Pacific Oceans by the Way of the Isthmus of Tehuantepec," Washington: Government Printing Office, 1872.

p. 25
Source: New Mexico History Museum, Santa Fe, NM

p. 26
E. A. Hayt, "Annual Report of the Commissioner of Indian Affairs, for the Year 1886" Office of Indian Affairs, U.S. Government Printing Office, 1886

p. 35
Jeff Hull, "Idea Lab, The Noises of Nature," New York Times, February 18, 2007

p. 37
Theodore Roosevelt, Letter to the President of the American Defense Society, January 3, 1919

p. 42
John Lankford, "The Lesson of Canal Zone Sanitation," Popular Science Monthly and World's Advance," Volume 83, 1913

p. 59
Source: Joongang Ilbo, March 17, 2010

p. 65-66
Carlisle Indian School Digital Resources Center, Dickinson College, http://carlisleindian.dickinson.edu/

p. 72
this sound

p. 91
feeling of safety

Earlier versions of some of these poems have appeared in *Hambone, Poetry, Best Experimental American Poetry 2016*, and *Interval(le)s*.

Myung Mi Kim is the author of *Penury* (Omnidawn), *Commons* (University of California), *DURA* (Sun and Moon, Nightboat Books), *The Bounty* (Chax Press), and *Under Flag* (Kelsey St. Press), winner of The Multicultural Publisher's Exchange Award of Merit. Her work has been anthologized in *Moving Borders: Three Decades of Innovative Writing by Women*, *Premonitions: Kaya Anthology of New Asian North American Poetry*, *American Hybrid: A Norton Anthology of New Poetry*, *American Poets in the 21st Century: The New Poetics*, and other collections. Magazine and journal publications include appearances in *Hambone*, *Sulfur*, *Conjunctions*, *How(ever)*, *Poetry*, *Interval(le)s: CIPA (Centre Interdisciplinaire de Poétique Appliquée)*, and *Cross-Cultural Poetics*. She has received fellowships and honors from the Fund for Poetry, the Djerassi Resident Artists Program, Gertrude Stein Awards in Innovative North American Poetry, and the State University of New York Chancellor's Award for Excellence in Scholarship and Creative Activity. Kim was born in Seoul, Korea and immigrated to the US at the age of nine. She is the James H. McNulty Chair of English at the University at Buffalo.